The Mass Book for Children

Rosemarie Gortler & Donna Piscitelli

Illustrated by Mimi Sternhagen

Our Sunday Visitor Publishing Division
Our Sunday Visitor, Inc.
Huntington, Indiana 46750

Nihil Obstat: Reverend Paul F. deLadurantaye
Censor Librorum

Imprimatur: Most Reverend Paul S. Loverde
Bishop of Arlington
July 9, 2004

Scripture citations, unless otherwise noted, are adapted from the *Catholic Edition of the Revised Standard Version of the Bible* (RSV), copyright © 1965, 1966 by the Division of Christian Education of the National Council of Churches of Christ in the United States of America. Used by permission. .

Excerpts from the English translation of *The Roman Missal* © 2010, International Commission on English in the Liturgy Corporation, Inc. All rights reserved.

Our Sunday Visitor Publishing Division
Our Sunday Visitor, Inc.
200 Noll Plaza
Huntington, IN 46750

ISBN: 978-1-59276-075-6 (Inventory No. T126)

Cover design by Monica Haneline
Cover and interior art by Mimi Sternhagen
Interior design by Sherri L. Hoffman

PRINTED IN UNITED STATES OF AMERICA

Graphics TwoFortyFourInc. Wheaton, IL USA
June 2014   LT 83225

Contents

The Mass Begins!

Look down the center aisle!
    Everybody stands up
        as the priest and altar servers
            walk to the altar of God.

It's like a parade!

When they are near the altar,
    Father bows very low.

Why does he do this?

He is *venerating* the altar of God.
Venerating means showing God
      a lot of loving respect
          — from deep in his heart.

Then they *genuflect* to the tabernacle.

Genuflecting means bowing down on one knee.
By genuflecting, they are recognizing
Jesus' presence in the tabernacle.

Then I will go to the altar of God, to God
my exceeding joy: and I will praise Him.
(Psalm 43:4)

Then Father walks around the altar,
    and kisses the altar!

Isn't that a funny thing to do?

Not really.
The altar is not an ordinary table.
It symbolizes Jesus!

The altar is where the sacrifice of Calvary
    takes place anew.
That's why Father kisses the altar.
Father is greeting his Friend to whom he has
    given his life!

The miracle of the Mass is an
    amazing act of love.

Let the word of Christ dwell in you richly.
(Colossians 3:16)

The Introductory Rite

After kissing the altar,
    Father walks to his chair,
        faces us,
            and makes the
                Sign of the Cross.
        "In the name of the Father,
        and of the Son,
        and of the Holy Spirit."

Why does he do this?
Catholics begin prayer
    with this simple act,
        an act of faith in the Trinity.

And the Mass is the *greatest act of faith.*

Then Father opens his arms wide to greet us.
He greets us as a father greets his children,
        blessing us
            with the grace and peace
                of Jesus Christ.

This greeting begins our conversation with God.

The Penitential Rite

When we go to see someone we really love,
  we get ready!

We wash our faces and hands
   and put on our good clothes.

Now we're at Mass!
   We have to get ready! How?
We pray a confession of our sins.

We ask God to purify our hearts
and we ask the saints, the angels,
     and our Blessed Mother
       to pray for us.
       And guess what?
They listen!
And they really do pray for us!
This is how we get ready
   to hear God's word.

♥

All Scripture is inspired by God and profitable
for teaching. (2 Timothy 3:16-17)

The Liturgy of the Word

Story time!

We sit down to hear a story
     from the Old Testament.

God talks to us in these stories
     about Noah, Moses,
and all the other people who lived
     before Christ was born.

We learn that God made us.
     We learn how He always
       watches over us.

These stories remind us of
     God's great love for us!

Next, we answer God
     by singing the Psalm together.

In many and various ways God spoke of old
to our fathers by the prophets.
(Hebrews 1:1-2)

The Psalms are the same prayers
    that Jesus prayed!
Did you know that the Psalms
    were written as love songs to God?

So we sing the Psalms,
    rejoicing in God's greatness
        and in our love for Him.

In the *second* reading
    God speaks to us again.

This time He talks to us
    in the stories we hear
        from the New Testament.

We hear the stories written by
    the apostles and disciples.

The apostles and disciples were friends
    with Jesus.
They walked and talked with Him.

Their letters and stories
    teach us how to stay close to Jesus.

Alleluia!
(Revelation 19:1)

The Gospel

Now comes the most important reading —
    the **Gospel.**

The **Gospel** is Jesus's own words.

With great respect,
    we all stand up to hear His words.

And…

Joyfully, we sing together
    the Great Alleluia!

"Alleluia, Alleluia, Alleluia!"

We sing this beautiful song because
    "Alleluia" means "Praise God!"

Praising God is a wonderful way to love Him.

And the Gospel must first be
preached to all nations.
(Mark 13:10)

15

The Gospel reading is *very important*,
  so only a priest or a deacon
    may read the Gospel at Mass.

Did you know that everyone
  in every Catholic church
    in the whole world
is hearing the same Gospel story on the same day?

Before reading the Gospel,
  Father makes the Sign of the Cross
    on the Book of the Gospel.

With his thumb he makes the Sign of the Cross
  on his forehead,
    on his lips, and over his heart.

And we all do the same thing, as we pray to ourselves:

**"The Lord be in my mind,
on my lips, and in my heart. Amen."**

Preach the word; be urgent in season
and out of season.
(2 Timothy 4:2-3)

When Father finishes reading the Gospel,
he kisses the Book of the Gospels
and quietly prays:

**"Through the words of the Gospel
may our sins be wiped away."**

Then we sit down to listen to Father's homily.
A homily is a talk by Father
that helps us understand the things
God is telling us.

Father explains how the words in the Bible
relate to our own lives.

We receive many graces
when we listen to the Gospel and the homily.

Hear my prayer, O God.
(Psalm 54:2)

The Profession of Faith

Everyone stands up again!
    Together we pray the Nicene Creed.

**"I believe in one God,
    the Father almighty,
        maker of heaven and earth…"**

The Nicene Creed is a very long prayer
    that talks about what we believe.

Next, we say the Prayer of the Faithful.
    All together
    we pray for the Church and for the whole world,
    we pray for people who are sick,
        for the souls of people who have died,
        and for anyone with special needs.

After each prayer everyone says:

"Lord, hear our prayer."

Praying for other people is a
wonderful act of love at Mass.

I will lift up the cup of salvation and
call on the name of the Lord.
(Psalm 116:13)

The Liturgy of the Eucharist

Get ready for the miracle!

Notice that people walk down the aisle to bring
gifts of bread and wine.
Then the altar servers help carry
         these gifts to the altar.

Watch what Father does.
         He takes the bread and wine
                  and places them on
                           a special cloth on the altar.

Why?

Because the bread and wine will become
         the **Body and Blood of Jesus.**

Father cannot allow
         the Body of Jesus
                  to be put just anywhere.

So, he uses a very special cloth.

I am the bread of Life.
(John 6:35)

Then Father picks up the bread
    on a special gold plate called a "paten."

He offers the bread to God,
        and he thanks God,
            and asks for God's blessing.
This bread will become the **Body of Christ.**

Then the altar server
    brings Father wine and water.

Father pours a small amount of water and wine
        into a special cup called the "chalice."
Then he prays,
"By the mystery of this water and wine
may we come to share in the divinity of Christ,
who humbled himself to share in our humanity."

Next, Father offers the wine to God
        and asks for His blessing.
This wine will become the **Blood of Christ.**

We offer ourselves to God at this time, too.
What a wonderful act of love at Mass.

Let us offer to God acceptable worship,
with reverence and awe.
(Hebrews 12:28)

Now Father washes his hands
as he says a prayer:

**"Wash me, O Lord, from my iniquity
and cleanse me from my sin."**

Why does he do this?
He must be sure he is as clean as he can be
before he handles
the Body and Blood of Jesus.

Then Father asks God to bless the bread and wine,
and we pray with him this wonderful prayer:

**"May the Lord accept the sacrifice at your hands
for the praise and glory of his name,
for our good
and the good of all his holy Church."**

In this prayer we are asking God
to accept the bread and wine Father is offering.
We are part of the miracle of God's love!

Participating in the Mass is a wonderful act of love.

Blessed is he who enters in the
name of the Lord!
(Psalm 118:26)

"Holy, Holy, Holy!"

It's time to rejoice,
    to lift up our hearts!

Everyone focuses on
    the wonderful miracle
        that is about to happen
            right in front of us!

We say this prayer of praise:

"Holy, Holy, Holy Lord God of hosts.
Heaven and earth are full of your glory.
Hosanna in the highest.
Blessed is he who comes in the name of the Lord.
Hosanna in the highest."

Remember when Jesus rode into Jerusalem
and the people lined the streets to greet Him?

They all sang His praises this same way!

Greeting Jesus this way is an act of reverence at Mass.

Holy, holy, holy is the Lord of hosts;
the whole earth is full of His glory.
(Isaiah 6:2-3)

Everyone, get on your knees!

The consecration is about to happen!
    This is the most solemn part of the Mass,
        so we pay close attention.

Father prays over the bread and wine
    and asks all the angels and saints
        to join us in our prayer to God.

Father asks the Holy Spirit to come
    and change this bread and wine into
        the Body and Blood of Jesus!

Watch carefully.
Father takes the bread in his hands
    and, lifting it up to God,
        he uses Jesus' own words:

**"TAKE THIS, ALL OF YOU, AND EAT OF IT,
FOR THIS IS MY BODY,
WHICH WILL BE GIVEN UP FOR YOU."**

Father holds the bread become Jesus up very high,
    showing it to all of us.

At that moment,
    all the angels in heaven are rejoicing!
        We bow our heads
            and offer a prayer
                to our great God.

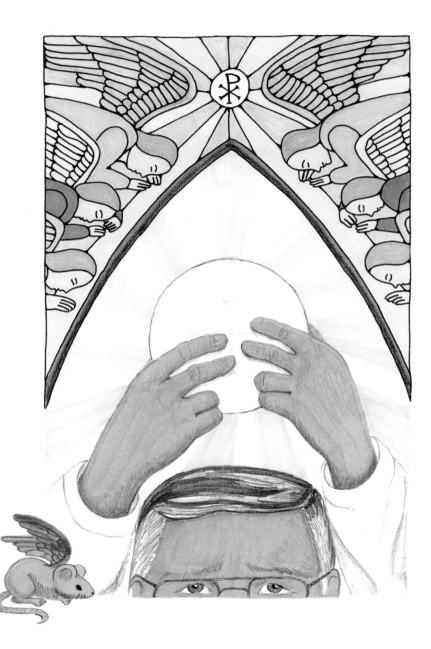

Then Father takes the chalice of wine.
Again he says the words Jesus spoke.

"TAKE THIS, ALL OF YOU, AND DRINK FROM IT,
FOR THIS IS THE CHALICE OF MY BLOOD,
THE BLOOD OF THE NEW AND ETERNAL COVENANT,
WHICH WILL BE POURED OUT FOR YOU AND FOR MANY
FOR THE FORGIVENESS OF SINS.
DO THIS IN MEMORY OF ME."

Father holds the chalice up very high,
        offering it to God.

And once again,
        all the angels in heaven rejoice!
                And all the people
                        bow their heads very low.

A miracle has just happened!
        We have just witnessed
                the Last Supper all over again.

And Jesus is going to give us
His Body and Blood,
just like He promised He would!

When Jesus had spoken these words,
He lifted up His eyes to heaven.
(John 17:1)

The Mystery of Faith

What a miracle!
  God changed bread and wine
    into the **Body and Blood of Jesus**.

This is part of the mystery of our faith.

Though it is difficult to understand,
    Jesus did die.
    He rose from the dead
    and He will come again.
He is always with us.

He told us He is the Bread of Life
    and that He will be with us always.
He told us to eat His Body
    and drink His Blood
        in remembrance of Him.

So even though it looks like bread and wine,
    the Eucharist is really
        the Body and Blood of Jesus!

Jesus told us so!

Christ died and lived again.
(Romans 14:9)

The Great Amen!

Holding the
Body and Blood of Jesus
high enough for all of us to see,
Father proclaims:

**"Through him, and with him, and in him,
O God, almighty Father,
in the unity of the Holy Spirit,
all glory and honor is yours,
for ever and ever."**

Then we all say, **"Amen!"**
which means **"Yes!"**

We stand up.
The miracle of the altar
has just happened
in front of our very eyes!

Jesus has come as He promised —
so we can receive Him!

For from Him and through Him and to Him are all
things. To Him be glory for ever. Amen.
(Romans 11:36)

The Communion Rite

Jesus's Real Presence is with us.
So now we pray
    the most perfect prayer —
        the one Jesus taught us to pray:

We all know this powerful prayer:

**"Our Father, who art in heaven,
hallowed be thy name;…"**

Why do we say this perfect prayer?

Because we recognize that we are God's children,
    no matter how old we are,
        and we want to obey His Will.

After saying Jesus' "Perfect Prayer,"
    Father offers us the peace of Jesus.

Then he asks us to offer Jesus' peace to each other
    before we receive the Body and Blood of Jesus,
        the Prince of Peace.

See what love the Father has given us, that we
should be called children of God; and so we are.
(1 John 3:1)

The Breaking of the Bread

Now Father breaks the Eucharist
    and puts a tiny piece of it into the chalice.

Why does he do this?

This is the mingling of the
    Body and Blood of Jesus.

As Father does this, we repeat a prayer
asking Jesus to take away
    all the sins in the world
        and to grant us peace.

Then we kneel and pray to God:

**"Lord, I am not worthy that you should enter under my roof,
but only say the word and my soul shall be healed."**

We know that God can
    and will heal us.
We only have to ask Him.

Now we are ready to receive the miracle!

Behold, the Lamb of God, who takes
away the sin of the world!
(John 1:29)

Everyone who has received
First Holy Communion
and wants to receive now
lines up with folded hands.

We pray as we walk
to receive this sacrament, **the Body of Christ.**
We bow before we receive.
What an important source of grace at Mass!

WOW!

After we receive the Eucharist,
we have the **Living Jesus** inside of us!

How close we are to Jesus!
This is an important time to pray,
telling Jesus all of our concerns,
and singing His praise.

He will hear us!

Great indeed, we confess,
is the mystery of our religion.
(1 Timothy 3:16)

The Concluding Rite

Watch Father now.
He is very careful to clean
    all the vessels he used for Communion.

He rinses everything out with water;
    then he drinks the water.

He won't allow any of Jesus'
    Body or Blood to be discarded.

So, out of reverence,
    Father drinks and eats
        any remaining particles.

Then Father invites us to stand.
    He gives us a blessing with hands
        that raised bread and wine to heaven.
    He gives us a blessing with hands
        that received Jesus'
                Body and Blood.

Blessed be the name of God for ever and ever.
(Daniel 2:20)

Remember how Jesus told His disciples to go
        and spread God's word to the whole world?

Father repeats Jesus' command.
He says, **"Go in peace."**

And now that we have received
        the **Body and Blood of Jesus,**
        we carry Jesus's Real Presence
        inside of us and out into the world with us.
We are living tabernacles!

Father lines up with all the altar servers.
They process out of the church,
        just like they came in.

Just like a parade!

They carry the processional crucifix
        out of the church,
        just like we will carry Jesus
        out into the world.
We go with peaceful hearts and loving smiles.

Go in peace.
(Luke 7:50)

Dear Parents:

This little book was especially written to help children understand the joy, the beauty, and the wonder of our Catholic Mass. We wrote it to encourage children to marvel at Christ's gift of the Eucharist, and His great sacrifice on the Cross.

Here's hoping that our children will appreciate the miracle of the Mass and continue to seek the love and peace that only God can give.

Fondly,
Rosemarie Gortler and Donna Piscitelli

ROSEMARIE GORTLER is an R.N. and licensed professional counselor. She is also an extraordinary minister of the Eucharist, a member of the Secular Franciscan Order, and a volunteer for Project Rachel. She and her husband, Fred, have five children and nineteen grandchildren.

DONNA PISCITELLI is a school administrator in Fairfax, Virginia. She is active in her church and in Christian outreach. She and her husband, Stephen, have four children and ten grandchildren.

MIMI STERNHAGEN is a home-school teacher and mother of five children. She and her husband, Don, assist with Family Life ministry in their parish. In addition to her collaborated works with Rosemarie and Donna, Mimi has illustrated *Catholic Cardlinks: Patron Saints* and *Teach Me About Mary*.

The authors extend their gratitude to Father Donald Rooney of St. Mary's Catholic Church in Fredericksburg, Virginia, and Father Francis De Rosa of St. Louis Catholic Church in Alexandria, Virginia, for their assistance in the preparation of this book.